FROM TALBOT TO STIEGLITZ

MASTERPIECES OF EARLY PHOTOGRAPHY FROM THE NEW YORK PUBLIC LIBRARY

Julia Van Haaften

THAMES AND HUDSON

Library of Congress Catalog Card Number 81-52310

ISBN 0-500-54077-2

Designed by Janet Doyle

Printed in the United States of America by Eastern Press

Contents ──────────────── ⫻

Preface ⟋⟋

"It will no more be possible to do without photography than without the printing press."
—1860 review of Francis Frith's *Egypt and Palestine Photographed and Described*

THE TRUTH OF THAT PROPHECY was evident before the century was out as photographs became the most common form of illustration in books and magazines. And, combined with the printed word or on their own, photographs have long been an important part of The New York Public Library's holdings.

Libraries have collected photographs primarily as illustrations and visual documents, not as works of art. Nevertheless, the great function of libraries as conservators of all they collect has guaranteed the survival (and made possible the rediscovery) of many rare and beautiful early photographs. *From Talbot to Stieglitz* celebrates this ongoing discovery at The New York Public Library. It also marks the establishment of the Research Libraries' first official department for photography, the newly organized Art, Prints & Photographs Division.

The Library is especially grateful for the enthusiastic support of Sandra Payson for the development of not only the exhibition and catalogue but also for assistance in enabling the Research Libraries to discover and make accessible its wide range of photographs. She has thus continued a family tradition of benefactions to the Library which began with her great-granduncle, Colonel Oliver Payne. We also must acknowledge the help of the Library staff who brought knowledge, excitement, and enthusiasm to this extensive work on our photographic collections.

Andrew Heiskell
Chairman of the Board of Trustees
The New York Public Library

Introduction ———————————— ⁄⁄⁄

THE HISTORY OF PHOTOGRAPHY was not seriously studied until 1937, when the centenary of the invention of photography was celebrated, and sustained research into archives and repositories has come into its own only in the last decade. In this short period, however, there has been a virtual explosion of information, as long forgotten photographs have been rediscovered, pioneers of the early days have been identified, and the various stages in the phenomenal development of photography have been reassessed.

The images presented in this book are all drawn from photographic collections in the Research Libraries of The New York Public Library. A few of the photographs are extremely famous, while others are completely unknown to modern viewers. They all reflect the Library's nineteenth-century origins and nearly universal collecting policy. Beginning with Fox Talbot, who invented photography on paper, and concluding with Alfred Stieglitz, who championed photography as an art medium, the book draws on the work of thirty-eight important photographers and spans eighty years with silver and platinum prints, collotypes, and photogravures. The selection demonstrates the range of master photographs at The New York Public Library and brings to a new and larger audience this internationally important collection.

William Henry Fox Talbot and Alfred Stieglitz—two creative and influential giants in the history of photography—provide ideal intellectual and chronological mileposts, for they represent respectively the very beginnings of photography in the late 1830s and its turn to modernism in the 1910s. During this period the world and its people became familiar to millions via the photograph. In a variety of formats—album views and portraits, postal cards, stereographs and published illustrations—photographs by and large came to mean "reality recorded" to nineteenth-century viewers. Even today a large part of the pleasure in looking at early photographs is the undeniable attraction of their rich and varied subject matter. Yet, from photography's earliest days it was also clear (to sensitive practitioners and audiences at least) that this most literal of pictorial media could be viewed subjectively, and could, like other graphic arts, convey mood, feeling, and tone.

Up to now, the history of photography has concentrated on photographers and technical processes, but an emerging area of critical inquiry is photography's subject matter. Nineteenth-century photography's primary concern was with content, and the medium's early viewers wondered at the clarity with which the physical world was rendered and transformed through a silver salt emulsion on a sheet of paper. For modern viewers, the beauty of nineteenth-century photographs endures not only in their capacity as records, but in their revelatory and evocative power as well.

A great photograph first tells the viewer something of the true physical reality of the subject—its texture, its shape, its solidity. It then goes beyond, to something that compels the viewer's attention: a gesture, a singularity of light, a compositional grace. In effect, all great photographs contain this duality of information and experience, of specific and universal. Their compelling physical reality—their awesome power to communicate—exists within an aura of persuasive emotional truth.

I. The Photographers

In 1835, the Englishman William Henry Fox Talbot invented the negative-positive system of photography, which he called "photogenic drawing." He continued to improve upon his unpublished achievement in the privacy of his country home, only to be staggered by Louis Daguerre's triumphant 1839 announcement of his own distinct discovery of photography on metal plates. Daguerreotypes, however, did not lend themselves to multiple or repeat images; each was a unique "positive" picture, a singular end result in itself. Talbot's "photogenic drawing," on

Note: The arrangement of plates parallels this discussion of photographers and their work.

the other hand, began with a negative image (lights were dark, darks light, and the image reversed as in a mirror), from which, he soon realized, any number of positive prints could be made.

The earliest photogenic drawings were made without a camera. To produce Plate 1, a leaf was placed against sensitized paper and exposed to sunlight, which darkened the uncovered area of the sheet, forming a "negative." When stabilized to prevent further reaction with light, this negative was placed over another sensitized sheet of paper and again exposed to sunlight. The second sheet darkened beneath the light areas of the negative and stayed light under the negative's darkened portions. Astonishingly simple, Talbot's revolutionary discovery theoretically permitted the infinite reproduction of nature's image. The negative became in effect the equivalent of the etcher's plate and the lithographer's stone.

Talbot devised small cameras at first and later larger ones to hold sensitized paper upon which rays of light were focused. By slow steps, involving chemical readjustments and an understanding of the action of light upon these chemicals to produce a latent image rather than a visible one, Talbot reduced original exposure times from hours to seconds. Even so, compared to the exquisitely detailed silver daguerreotype, Talbotypes (for so he patented his process) seemed muddy and dull in the public view. Despite the publication of Talbot's explanatory volume, *The Pencil of Nature* (1844–46), it took ten more years and the technical improvements of others for the significance of photography's potential as a fine graphic-arts medium to be grasped fully.

REGIONAL PHOTOGRAPHY

Early photographers found both city and countryside obvious sources of photographic subjects. In the United States, the Philadelphia-based Langenheim brothers helped arouse the public's appetite for stereoscopic travel views with their handsome and original series of hand-colored glass views depicting Niagara Falls in winter and summer (1854–55). By 1850, albumen on glass was replacing paper as a base for negatives, resulting in a highly detailed image, and these translucent glass stereos gave the viewer the illusion of being right on the edge of the Falls. The ability of early stereographs to simulate the dramatic aspects of distant locales was the format's chief attraction. Other areas visited and photographed by cameraman William Langenheim and his brother Frederick during the mid-1850s include the Pennsylvania coal region and New York City.

Victor Prevost had been a minor Parisian lithographer before coming to New York in 1848, but by 1853 he was working as a photographer. His views, made from waxed-paper negatives (a step toward the transparency of glass), are among the earliest surviving photographs of New York City streets and architecture. Prevost's other famous series, made on glass negatives in 1862, shows the new Central Park. In these images, the landscape seems raw, the architecture stark, and the figures have a nature-disdaining, urbane bearing. Although the commercial photographer George Rockwood was the officially licensed photographer for the park, Prevost received special permission to produce his thirty-print portfolios, as the blind-stamp on each of his mounts very clearly states.

On the Continent, the Alinaris and Édouard Baldus were among the most prolific urban photographers of the 1850s. Alinari Fratelli—the famous Florentine photo archive and art-reproduction firm—was founded in 1854 by cameraman Leopoldo Alinari and his brother Giuseppe, with the financial backing of the printseller Luigi Bardi. Their first undertaking was a series of large views depicting their native Tuscany and its works of art. Photographed with albumenized glass plates, the rich landscapes and architectural studies were printed on an albumen paper that produced a deep velvety texture yet permitted accurate transmission of all the detail in the negatives. These photographs were sold on mounts bearing only Luigi Bardi's blind-stamp as publisher. Leopoldo's early death in 1865 and the loss of his sensitive vision seem to have caused the firm to turn its efforts away from interpretive landscapes and cityscapes toward a more documentary approach to art history.

Édouard Baldus, a founding member of the Société Héliographique, was one of several French photographers (including Gustave Le Gray, Henri Le Secq, and Hippolyte Bayard) commissioned by the Comité des Monuments Historiques to document historic French architecture in 1851–52. His assignment was Paris (in addition to Fontainebleau, Burgundy, and the Dauphiné), a responsibility that made his reputation as the leading French architectural photographer of his day, and prepared him for his later self-initiated surveys of the capital city. While his earliest efforts were undertaken with waxed-paper or gelatine-paper negatives, his later views (reproduced here) were made with the wet-collodion process and printed on albumen paper. Baldus also completed a thorough survey of the Louvre's new wing in 1854–55 and photographed along the recently opened Paris-Marseilles and Paris-Calais rail routes. In his later years, Baldus' continued interest in heliography, a high-quality photo-mechanical process, led him to publish among other works a multi-volume set of his Versailles views using that method.

Robert Mieusement was another French architectural photographer given to making surveys, in Baldus' tradition if not quite with his style. Mieusement's several-volume *Chateaux historiques* series of 1875 records in a workmanlike manner the restoration of major castles in the Loire Valley. Scattered examples of his work with ecclesiastical architecture have come to light, but it is the consistently straightforward record of the chateaux series which makes this otherwise obscure photographer noteworthy.

Alvin Langdon Coburn's photographs of architecture and city scenes are very much of the twentieth century. Welcomed to the world of photography while still in his teens by his cousin, the pictorial photographer F. Holland Day, Coburn met Henry James in 1905 while in New York on a magazine assignment to photograph the famous author. James liked young Coburn immediately and a year later, after mulling over the question of frontispieces for the definitive edition of his works, proposed a collaboration for the requisite twenty-plus images. Coburn set off for Paris and Venice armed with James' detailed instructions on what to photograph and where to find it. As to *how* to photograph, James trusted Coburn's ability to produce, in the words of James' biographer, "optical symbols" that would enhance rather than intrude upon James' own literary images. James personally led Coburn on walking tours around the London neighborhoods of his younger days in search of remembered sites and details.

Despite James' contention that photographs would have an objectivity, an impersonal quality that drawings and paintings lack, the frontispieces definitely reflect Coburn's characteristic interest in composition and viewpoint. A member of Alfred Stieglitz' Photo-Secession and its English counterpart, The Linked Ring, Coburn championed photogravure as a modern printmaking technique and published several series of his own photographs (*New York*, 1910; *London*, 1914; *Men of Mark*, 1913), pulling his gravures on a press in his London studio.

DOCUMENTARY PHOTOGRAPHY

The events and faces of the times have always been natural subjects for the camera's witnessing eye. While not the earliest war to be photographed, the American Civil War was the first to be so thoroughly documented. "Instantaneous" pictures still took several seconds' exposure, which effectively prohibited action shots. Nevertheless, photographers traveled with soldiers in special field wagons where they could set up their cumbersome wet-collodion cameras and process their plates.

Already versed in photography when he arrived in America from Scotland in 1856, Alexander Gardner managed Mathew Brady's Washington gallery until 1863 when he opened his own studio in reaction to Brady's unwillingness to permit his cameramen individual credit for their images. A follower of Robert Owen and a Swedenborgian, Gardner hoped his hundred-print *Photographic Sketch Book of the War* would have some influence for peace:

> Verbal presentations of such places, or scenes, may or may not have the merit of accuracy; but photographic presentments of them will be accepted by posterity with an undoubting faith . . . Here are the dreadful details! Let them aid in preventing another such calamity falling upon the nation.

His view of the stark silhouette of a bombed-out arsenal attests to the anonymous destructive power of modern war as surely as his portrait of the handsomely dressed officers is proof of man's sad willingness to wage it.

Gardner took two photographers from Brady's operation with him when he started his own studio—Timothy H. O'Sullivan and George N. Barnard. O'Sullivan, who was barely in his twenties when the Civil War began, photographed at every major engagement of the Army of the Potomac, first for Mathew Brady and later with Alexander Gardner. Perhaps Gardner's antiwar sentiment influenced O'Sullivan's photographs at Gettysburg (his first work after the split with Brady). With its unrelieved horizon line, O'Sullivan's grim long view of the corpse-strewn, smoky battlefield is an abstract, unsentimentalized, and horrifying record of death.

Toward the end of the Civil War, former daguerreotypist George N. Barnard was dispatched from the chief engineer's office of the Division of the Mississippi to accompany General William T. Sherman on his invasion of the deep South. From Tennessee through the "War-is-hell" general's devastating march to the sea, Barnard's *Photographic Views of Sherman's Campaign* communicate the stillness and the finality of the South's utter defeat.

A reunified America responded eagerly to France's proposed gift of a statue symbolizing liberty. Sculptor Auguste Bartholdi designed the figure, while engineer Gustave Eiffel devised *Liberty*'s cast-iron strapwork core to support her one-eighth-inch-thick skin of hammered copper. The statue was

actually built in Paris over a period of four years, and *Liberty*—completely assembled—was presented to the United States in 1883. Albert Fernique, an engineer by training who specialized in technical subjects, photographed the statue as it was being built, and can be considered one of the first industrial photographers.

By the turn of the century, America was experiencing a swell of European immigration. Alfred Stieglitz' much-reproduced 1907 photograph "The Steerage" is frequently thought to be the result of a New York dockside visit. However, it is a scene serendipitously caught by Stieglitz while on a ship bound from New York to Europe:

> I stood spellbound for a while. I saw shapes related to one another—a picture of shapes, and underlying it, a new vision that held me: simple people; the feeling of the ship, ocean, sky; a sense of release.

The image was published first in *Camera Work* in October 1911, and again four years later in a larger format in Stieglitz' art journal *291*.

It's not improbable that some of the passengers in Stieglitz' "Steerage" were rejected would-be immigrants being returned to their ports of embarkation. Augustus Francis Sherman, the chief registry clerk at Ellis Island and an amateur photographer, had plenty of opportunities to pose and record potential new citizens during the frequent delays in processing. His subjects embody the hope, courage, and determination necessary to begin life in a new land. While Sherman's photography during the ten peak years of immigration before World War I was not an official Immigration Service duty, the department did furnish his photographs to *National Geographic* and other publications to help tell the story of Ellis Island.

But it is through the crusading photography of Lewis Hine that the immigrants' experience in America has best been preserved. Hine, a schoolteacher, began photographing at Ellis Island in 1904, and later traveled throughout the industrial regions of the United States to factories and mills, recording both the scandalous conditions of child labor and the heroic quality of all labor. Working people and their environments remained his life-long subjects, culminating in a lyrical essay in 1930 on the construction of the Empire State Building. Hine was unable to find employment during the Depression, not even with the Farm Security Administration's army of documentary cameramen, and it was only in the last years of his life that this gentle, dedicated photographer received recognition as the progenitor of the American documentary tradition.

EXPLORATION

The photographs brought back by early expeditionary cameramen—like those from outer space in our own time—were received as revelations by their eager audiences. Not only were they astonishing in terms of detail and composition, they were also remarkable for their technical success. All of the complex manipulations necessary to produce a single negative—sensitizing, developing, washing—had to be carried out on the spot, in spite of heat, cold, dust, damp, insects, and animals, all of which seemed to conspire to ruin plates and spoil chemicals.

Because photographic enlargements were impracticable, the size of the negative determined the size of the print. For the largest views, called mammoth (up to 560 x 630 mm), large sheets of glass and furniture-sized cameras were necessary; the sheer physical feat of transporting and handling such cumbersome equipment successfully is still admirable.

Egypt and the Holy Land—exotic and rich in religious associations—were major goals for early exploring photographers. Within a decade of each other, a Frenchman, Maxime Du Camp, and an Englishman, Francis Frith, made separate and thorough photographic records of their long and sometimes arduous journeys through what are now Egypt, Israel, Lebanon, and Syria. Du Camp, traveling with his friend the young Gustave Flaubert (whose diaries of the trip curiously contain but few references to Du Camp's photography), used a modification of Talbot's paper-negative process on his 1849–51 tour of the Middle East's historic monuments. His photo-illustrated book of the tour is one of the earliest and largest of such publications in France, containing 122 soft, gold-toned albumen prints from Blanquart-Evrard's photo-printing firm in Lille. With their tight framing and narrow field of vision, Du Camp's photographs invite a close intimacy with the ruins.

Francis Frith followed Du Camp to the Middle East in 1856, and by 1860 had made three separate trips. More concerned with vistas and the dramatic modeling of forms by the harsh desert sunlight, Frith's views are less personal than Du Camp's but do give more information about the land and its monuments. While Du Camp traveled ostensibly under the authority of the French ministry of education, Frith journeyed independently in a canvas-covered photographic wagon. After each trip, he sold the rights to his stereographs and mammoth views, while reserving the medium-size prints for his own numerous publications, including two Bibles. He eventually became the largest view publisher in England and was able to assign hired cameramen to photograph locally and abroad for postcards and album views; F. Frith & Co. was in business until 1968.

Greece was a popular destination of nineteenth-century travelers, although it seems to have been less favored than the Middle East by photographers. D. Constantin, whose biography is obscure, was a native Greek photographer who worked for the travel-view market. Despite this commercial impetus, he was a skillful cameraman, and his compositions reflect an appreciation of the romantic drama of Athens' classical sites.

Désiré Charnay was one of the first to successfully photograph the overgrown ruins of the pre-Columbian Yucatan. Struggling with oppressive heat and humidity in the tropical forests between 1857 and 1859, Charnay produced a series of elegant large-format views which Blanquart-Evrard printed as an atlas with a text by Charnay and an introduction by architectural historian Viollet-le-Duc. Charnay's Yucatan series conveys a strong sense of abandonment and decay, as do Du Camp's views of Egypt, and is an invaluable record of the pre-archaeological period.

Early photographers were also tempted by exotic locations closer to home. Founding members of the Société Française Photographique, the Bisson Frères began as daguerreotypists in Paris and by the 1850s were specializing in large-format paper photographs of architectural subjects. Between 1855 and 1868 they made several expeditions to the Alps and attempted to scale Mont Blanc at least once before producing successful images in 1861 and 1862. The photographs show sweeping glacial vistas and abstract, sculptural curves of snow accented by the figures of the Bissons' climbing companions.

For North Americans, the unexplored West was the expeditionary photographer's goal. The Great Desert, the Rockies, and the areas that were to become Yellowstone, Yosemite, and Grand Canyon National Parks were all photographed extensively during the 1860s and 1870s.

In the late 1850s, Charles L. Weed became the first to photograph in the Yosemite Valley, and he was followed closely by his contemporary and fellow daguerreotypist Carleton E. Watkins. The two rivals sold their photos mounted and signed like fine prints to a clientele eager to champion the natural wonders of America. Watkins' grand landscapes—instrumental in the successful passage of a bill signed by President Lincoln preserving Yosemite—are practically devoid of human figures or any other evidence of the hand of man, while Weed on occasion tucks a figure or two into a pocket in the landscape, defying the rugged terrain with a picturesque convention. The realism and grandeur of the country as seen in these photographs parallel contemporary trends in American landscape painting.

A. J. Russell also used figures to supply scale and meaning

to the bizarre rock formations and railroad cuts he documented as official photographer for the Union Pacific Railroad's transcontinental effort following the Civil War. The railroad route was already surveyed and track laid down when Russell began to record what was in essence a public-relations campaign for the opening of the West. Issued in fifty-print albums, Russell's images comprise the first photographs of sights that became familiar landmarks to generations of transcontinental railroad travelers.

The conditions for photographers attached to the government surveys of the late 1860s and 1870s were quite different from Russell's established route and pre-planned photography. The very purpose of the surveys was to document uncharted country, aid in mapping, and record geological phenomena for future study. Civil War cameraman Timothy O'Sullivan accompanied several expeditions to the West, including Clarence King's. His photographs disdain all conventions that might lead the eye into a picture, and emphasize the vastness and the harsh inaccessibility of the West.

In 1872, William Bell, a commercial photographer from Philadelphia and Baltimore (and not the English medical doctor William A. Bell who was photographing in the West at the same time), replaced O'Sullivan on Lieutenant George M. Wheeler's survey. Wheeler included photographs by both Bell and O'Sullivan in a fifty-print album supplied to members of Congress to encourage further appropriations for these military expeditions. Bell frequently composed his views with strong diagonals leading in from the lower or upper edges of the picture frame, and on occasion his work took on O'Sullivan's abstract qualities.

Contemporary with the photo surveys of the West was the 1869 expedition to Greenland by painter William Bradford and Arctic explorer Isaac Hayes, accompanied by two cameramen from J. W. Black's Boston studio, George Dunmore and John L. Critcherson. It seems likely that Bradford guided the photographers in their choice of subject and even in its interpretation; the subtitle of his lavish 1873 photo-illustrated book of views from this trip attests: "Illustrated with Photographs Taken on an Art Expedition . . ." Although Hayes' earlier Arctic voyages had produced stereoscopic views, Bradford's obsessive interest in the far north resulted in the earliest group of large-format views of the region and its people.

From the very beginning, India had been photographed by members of the British colonial service, but the most prominent and the most prolific photographer was a civilian, Samuel Bourne. Settling in Simla in 1861, he spent the next decade on the subcontinent, with studios in Bombay and Calcutta too. His several expeditions into the Himalayas—the largest with an army of bearers, furniture, and animals for food—made his reputation with wondrous views of the awesome range. Today, his exhaustive documentation of Indian architecture and monuments remains of special value.

John Thomson, a fellow of the Royal Geographical Society, set out on his first journey to the Far East in the 1860s. He photographed in Siam, Cambodia, Hong Kong, and the Malay Peninsula, and in 1867 published his Cambodian views; he used many of the other photographs as sources for wood engravings in later books of his travels. Best known for his monumental series on China (1873) and on London street life (1877–78), Thomson never did issue the Siam views in book form. Those reproduced here are from an album collected in 1868 by an American officer on a naval expedition to the South China Sea.

NATURAL HISTORY

The ability of the camera to faithfully record what is placed before it led quickly to photography's use in scientific documentation. In 1854 Talbot published a pamphlet with Talbotype illustrations of hieroglyphic inscriptions, and in that same year an American scientist, John C. Warren, issued a book on fossil impressions with a salt print bound-in as a frontispiece. Sixty years later, Edwin Hale Lincoln's New England wildflowers provide another example. His studio arrangements of plant specimens draw on a centuries-long tradition of fine botanical illustration.

Eadweard Muybridge, the English-born father of the motion picture, had a varied career in photography in America. He photographed in Yosemite after Watkins and Weed (and artistically his work surpasses theirs). He worked in Alaska, and in California during the Modoc Indian War, before engaging in the famous horse-gait investigations for Leland Stanford that launched his monumental *Animal Locomotion* study. Undertaken in 1884 and 1885 in Philadelphia, with the sponsorship of the University of Pennsylvania and the aid of Thomas Eakins, the painter, Muybridge's stop-action, sequential photographic studies were published in 1887 in eleven volumes of rich collotype plates as *Animal Locomotion, An Electro-Photographic Investigation of Phases of Animal Movements.* His initial studies of people and animals led him to develop the zoopraxiscope, a form of projector that showed line drawings adapted from his sequential photographs in apparent motion.

ETHNOLOGY AND GENRE

Both ethnological studies and genre photography were popular throughout the nineteenth century. Ethnological photographs were usually posed or arranged—not straight records in the modern anthropological sense—but they remain useful documents for interpretation. Genre or picturesque studies, meant to be examples of naturalism, can now be seen as valuable records of vanished ways of life, although they too require knowledgeable interpretation.

In the American West, early photographers, already sensing they were racing against the effects of modern forces on a traditional way of life, were still able to photograph a changing but unconquered people. John K. Hillers, the German-born boatman who became Major John Wesley Powell's photographer in 1873 during the Colorado River surveys, photographed Zuni, Hopi, and Navajo Indians in the Southwest, in lively individual portraits and in documentary architectural and ceremonial studies. In 1879 Powell became director of the new United States Bureau of Ethnology and appointed Hillers official photographer, their friendship ending only with Powell's death in 1902.

Edward S. Curtis is surely the best-known photographer of the American Indian. His ambitious project—a comprehensive and interpretive record of American Indian tribes—was completed in 1930 after twenty-five years of intensive work, chiefly with the financial support of financier J. P. Morgan and his estate. *The North American Indian* consists of twenty illustrated volumes and their accompanying portfolios of larger gravure plates. Curtis' photographs, rich sources now for investigative ethnologists, are always hauntingly beautiful. Despite their soft texture and pictorialist presentations, the portraits and other figure studies have a dignity that goes beyond sentimentality. There is evidence that the Library's Curtis photographs—with price labels still attached to their mounts—were the photographer's first attempt to raise funds for his project at the turn of the century.

Karl E. Moon was an immigrant from Germany, like Hillers, who settled permanently in New Mexico early in this century. Enchanted with the picturesque qualities of the Indian way of life, Moon, an illustrator, turned his talent to making artistic photographs of Indian subjects for sale as fine prints, and produced portrait studies and occasional romanticized scenes. Moon abandoned photography in the 1910s and later collaborated with his wife for many years on children's books about Indian life.

Juan Laurent was based in Madrid and is one of the few Spanish cameramen from the early period of photography. Though he was known also for his straightforward architectural studies, Laurent's largest work was his *Museos de España,* a handsome series on Spanish character and occupations. The figures and compositions, though obviously staged to depict narrative situations, retain a liveliness that appears quite naturalistic.

In Japan, beginning in the 1860s and into this century, first foreign and then local photographers made genre studies of the Japanese people for the Western market. An elegant series of hand-colored albumen prints issued in Yokohama in 1869 are attributed to F. A. Beato, who had photographed in the Middle East during the 1850s before venturing to China and Japan. With their vignetted format, subject matter, and subtle coloring, Beato's photographs evoke the finest Japanese woodcuts, but they are entirely a Western convention and have no indigenous counterpart in Japanese photography. Eventually Beato settled permanently in Luxor and became the leading commercial Egyptian view photographer.

Frank M. Sutcliffe's life-long study of the traditional ways of life of the Channel-coast village of Whitby and its countryside contains some of the spirit that infuses the works of Edward Curtis. Though worlds apart in motivation and photographic aesthetic, both photographers recognized the vastness and irrevocability of the changes that modern technology would bring to centuries-old ways of life. Sutcliffe's sharp, naturalistic images from the 1880s and 1890s, though occasionally staged to illustrate a narrative scene, record people, harbor, and town as Sutcliffe, who lived in Whitby all his adult life, came to know them.

PORTRAITURE

Most of the photographs in the Research Libraries are portraits. The small selection here includes portraits that are not part of any of the great iconographic files within The New York Public Library.

Mathew Brady is best known as the photographer of Lincoln and the Civil War, but he was also the leading American portrait photographer of his time, with studios in New York and Washington. He specialized in portraits of the great and famous in the collectable *carte-de-visite* format and in stereographs. The P. T. Barnum–promoted wedding of Tom Thumb in 1863 is a prime example of the celebrity subjects Brady photographed in order to finance his survey of the Civil War. Yet Brady was regarded as a fellow artist by contemporary painters and collectors; his group portrait with the Art Committee of the 1864 New York Metropolitan Fair includes painters Albert Bierstadt, John Kensett, Daniel Huntington, Eastman Johnson, and Emmanuel Leutze, architect Richard Morris Hunt, dealer M. Knoedler, and photographer-scientist Lewis Morris Rutherfurd, who are pictured posing with relevant art work while Brady appropriately faces the camera.

Étienne Carjat was a French counterpart and contemporary of Brady. Carjat's early background as a caricaturist and journalist ensured his success in portraiture, while his unflinching study of Charles Baudelaire (who despised the shoddiness of commercial portrait photography) placed him artistically alongside such masters as the famed Nadar.

Photography, more than any other art, has had its share of amateur practitioners, and eminent among them was the Irish playwright George Bernard Shaw. Shaw took up photography with the advent of push-button cameras in 1898, and was soon adopted by the photographers of the English pictorialist circle, The Linked Ring. The group's American counterpart, Stieglitz' Photo-Secession, also welcomed the famous writer, who contributed articles to the early issues of *Camera Work*. Shaw obligingly posed for Alvin Langdon Coburn and in 1907 earned the title "The Photographer's Best Model" from Edward Steichen. He was also his own model in his earliest years in photography, sharing his self-portraits with his friend and fellow Linked Ring member Frederick H. Evans. In the 1920s and 1930s, Evans transmitted Shaw's photographs in letters to the art dealer and publisher Mitchell Kennerley.

It was also to Kennerley that Georgia O'Keeffe and Alfred Stieglitz sent Edward Steichen's portrait of Stieglitz and Stieglitz' photographs of O'Keeffe's hands. Steichen was a founding member of Stieglitz' Photo-Secession and belonged to the Linked Ring. His 1905 portrait of his mentor dates from the height of their association on *Camera Work* and in the influential "291" gallery. By the 1920s, Steichen was an established commercial photographer in fashion, advertising, portraiture, and publicity. He worked with the Army in World War I and later for the Navy in World War II, specializing in aerial operations and aviation subjects. From 1947 to 1962 Steichen directed the growing Photography Department for the Museum of Modern Art in New York, during which time he organized the renowned exhibition "The Family of Man."

The influence that Alfred Stieglitz has exerted as editor, photographer, and gallery operator on American art in this century is inestimable. Trained in photographic chemistry and experienced with commercial photogravure, Stieglitz first led the American photographic community as editor of the Camera Club of New York's increasingly pictorialist *Camera Notes*. He left this group in 1902 to found the famed Photo-Secession and its sumptuous journal *Camera Work*, which, in fifty issues from 1903 to 1917, championed the work of modern European and American artists. Beginning with a pictorialist aesthetic, Stieglitz changed his view to advocate the primacy of "straight"—that is, unretouched or tampered with—photography, and *Camera Work* reflects this transition. He later developed his theory of the photographic "equivalent," a spiritual and symbolic aesthetic.

Stieglitz made his earliest portraits of his future wife, the painter Georgia O'Keeffe, in 1917. That same year saw the last issue of *Camera Work* (with its radically different photographs by the young Paul Strand) and the last exhibition at "291," the second show of O'Keeffe's paintings. The "O'Keeffe hands" here are not portraits in the traditional sense; nor are they anonymous artistic studies, devoid of personality. They are in fact the only modern photographs in this selection because they reveal more about the artist and his vision than they do about his subject.

II. The Library

IN SIZE AND DIVERSITY, The New York Public Library's collection of original photographic prints ranks with those of the Library of Congress and the Bibliothèque Nationale. The national libraries' role of copyright depository ensured the encyclopedic nature of their collections. The New York Public lacked any such mission, yet over the years has come to hold an unusual—and partially buried—treasure trove of photographica. How this came about requires a look at photographic publishing and at the Library's history.

Photography on paper and photographic publishing are nearly synonymous. Indeed, the desire to print multiple images from just one camera exposure provided the impetus for the discovery of the negative-positive system of photography. Having announced his success with photography on paper in 1839, William Henry Fox Talbot from 1844 to 1846 issued *The Pencil of Nature*, a book-in-parts that illustrated his process with actual photographs mounted on the pages. In effect, he published the first of what has become an industry commonplace, a photographic book.

Within the decade following Talbot's discovery and publication, the Astor Library—from which The New York Public

Library is descended—was founded. It was only natural for such a modern and progressive institution, as was this first fully public library in New York, to collect contemporary photographic books. Today such rarities as Désiré Charnay's views of the Yucatan and Maxime Du Camp's views from the Middle East as well as the more modest historic chateaux series by Robert Mieusement are identified among the routine acquisitions of the Astor Library.

The Lenox Library—another parent—contributed many nineteenth-century photographs via its Robert L. Stuart Collection, a wonderful gentleman's library (which the N.Y.P.L. received when it agreed to close the collection to the public on Sundays). The personal library of the third benefactor, Samuel J. Tilden, also added photographs to the collections.

Most of the other photographica arrived after the 1911 opening of the Central Building on Fifth Avenue, and while many of the acquisitions are datable, their provenances are for the most part lost. Into the 1930s, gifts and purchases added primarily nineteenth-century material, including photographs by Talbot, Alinari, Baldus, and Curtis. Since then, the Library has collected contemporary as well as historical photographs, especially in the areas of biography, New York history, the performing arts, and social sciences. Notable recent acquisitions include an 1868 album containing John Thomson's views in Siam and two portfolios of mammoth views of Yosemite Valley by Carleton E. Watkins and Charles L. Weed.

Despite the word "Public" in its name, the Library is a private institution, made up of many special collections, branches, and research departments. Until 1980, the Library had no separate curatorial department for photographs, and as a result nearly every department in the Research Libraries developed, in one way or another, its own specialized collection of photographs. Archival collections, like the Manuscripts Division and the Berg Collection, acquired photographs as part of larger gifts and purchases of papers or documents. Albums of travel views and portraits were kept by the General Research & Humanities Division for use in the Main Reading Room. The Art & Architecture Division collected albums of architecture and costume studies and made up scrapbooks from loose photographs. Rarities that fit nowhere else went to the Rare Book Division. Concurrently, the Branch Libraries' Picture Collection—which had a very active photograph-acquisition program until the past decade's budget crisis—maintained a voluminous photograph file arranged by subject and/or photographer. Indeed, it is this collection that usually comes to mind when photographs at the Library are discussed.

Some of the Research Libraries' divisional collections are now world-famous. Well-organized and readily accessible, they include collections at Lincoln Center's Performing Arts Research

Center, the Schomburg Center for Research in Black Culture, and the Central Building on Fifth Avenue. Lincoln Center's Music Division has a massive iconographic file arranged by personality, ranging from *cartes-de-visite* of nineteenth-century opera greats to publicity glossies of last year's rock groups. The Theatre Collection's monumental archives contain movie stills, stage set documentation, publicity portraits, and related photographs, while the Dance Collection includes work by Arnold Genthe and Baron de Meyer among others. The Schomburg Center maintains a photo archive on Black life and personalities in the United States and abroad from the nineteenth century to the present. Cross-indexed by photographers' names and additional subjects, the collection includes work by Doris Ullmann and Gordon Parks.

The Central Building contains two large and long-established collections of original photographs—the Local History & Genealogy Division's "New York City and Environs" file and the Robert Dennis Collection of Stereoscopic Views. The former, arranged by New York City street addresses, goes back to the 1860s, but is especially strong from 1890 to the 1930s and includes work by the Wurts Brothers, Berenice Abbott, and Percy Sperr. The stereoscopic-view collection is a microcosm of the Research Libraries' photograph holdings in terms of diversity and photo technology. The views themselves, as ubiquitous in their age as television is in ours, are windows into the nineteenth century and reveal much about the way the age saw itself.

The above-mentioned collections are all well-known and accessible *as photographs.* Yet there are many smaller but fascinating photograph collections in the Research Libraries that—unrecognized, uncatalogued, or inaccessible—have been rediscovered only in the past few years. Occasionally hidden within larger archival holdings, and frequently entered in the Library's main card catalog as if they were textless books, these photographs have been the object of investigation by the Photograph Collections Documentation Project for the past two years.

We began the search by tracking down published books—like Talbot's *Pencil of Nature*—with actual photographic prints pasted-in, and located nearly five hundred titles within the Research Libraries' divisions. This initial effort provided a glimpse into the wealth of photographica remaining to be discovered, for in addition to illustrated books, the search unearthed portfolios and albums as well as photographs which had been made into scrapbooks in the Library's bindery half a century earlier. Some of these were entered in the Public Catalog and were assigned call numbers and subject headings similar to those for printed books on the same topics. Therefore, many of the nineteenth-century topographic photographs were entered under a place name and the subdivision "Views." Such was the case with the photos taken by the Bisson Frères of their daring ascent of Mont Blanc. The original stamped mounts had been trimmed and pasted into a volume entitled for cataloguing convenience *Scrapbook of Switzerland Views* Vol. 2; there was no additional entry for the Bissons. The anonymous gift of photographs by John Thomson and others of China and Southeast Asia had been catalogued under only one heading, "Far East—Views."

Real results were achieved by persistently visiting likely subject areas in the stacks and spotting un-booklike volumes on the shelves (severely wrinkled pages indicated lots of internal pasting), by alerting the rest of the Library's staff to report serendipitous photography finds, and by obsessively searching in the Public Catalog under likely geographical and ethnological headings. Binder's titles that began with the words "Album of . . .", "Collection of . . .", "Scrapbook of . . .", "Views of . . .", not to mention "Photographs . . .", were also fruitful areas in the Public Catalog. And careful perusal of the manuscript collections' inventories combined with clues from the staff produced other remarkable treasures (like the Steichen, Stieglitz, and Shaw photographs).

It is primarily from the discoveries produced by this effort that the images for *From Talbot to Stieglitz* have been drawn.

Julia Van Haaften
Director
Photograph Collections Documentation Project

For the success of the photo Project plus the happy existence of this celebratory volume and the exhibition it records I am grateful to many at the Library for their help and support: Sandra Payson, Phyllis Gordan, Sharon Frost, Alejandro Olivera, David H. Stam, Juanita Doares, Donald F. Anderle, Rodney Phillips, Michael Calvano and his staff, John P. Baker and his staff, Ana Loud Jones, Ruth Ann Stewart, and Bernard McTigue. I thank the entire staff of the new Art, Prints & Photographs Division as well as the wonderfully helpful staffs of all the other divisions for their cooperation during the course of the project. I also wish to acknowledge the contributions of all those at the Library who over the years have created or cared for photograph collections.

Other important supporters of the Photo Project were: Alan Fern, Library of Congress; Doris C. O'Neil and her colleagues at Time, Inc.; and Howard Gilman and Pierre Apraxine, Gilman Paper Company.

Grants from the National Endowment for the Arts and the National Endowment for the Humanities provided significant funding for the cataloguing work of the Photo Project upon which this publication has drawn.

And, without the aid and encouragement of my husband Ron Schick and the understanding of our daughter Madeline this book could not have been completed.

J.V.H.

Plates

1. William Henry Fox Talbot. [*Photogenic drawing of a plant*]. c. 1845.

The Talbot photographs shown here come from a larger group presented by Talbot to the French photo researcher Hippolyte Fizeau, which came to the Library in 1938.

2. William Henry Fox Talbot.   [*China on two shelves*].   c. 1841–1843.

This is one variation of several arrangements of china and glassware which Talbot photographed to demonstrate the camera's ability as a documentor or visual cataloguer.

3. William Henry Fox Talbot.   [*Nelson Column under construction,*
Trafalgar Square].   1845.

The comparatively long exposure time required precluded capturing
any of the workmen's activity.

4. William and Frederick Langenheim. *Niagara Falls . . . General View from American Side.* 1855.

The Langenheims issued their stereograph series with and without hand-coloring, in glass views and on paper. The figures in this view provide scale to the Falls.

5. William and Frederick Langenheim. *New York City and Vicinity. View from Peter Cooper's Institute towards Astor Place.* c. 1856.

6. Victor Prevost. *Central Park in 1862, No. 17: Bird's Nest [Bethesda Fountain Stairway].* 1862.

7. Victor Prevost. *Central Park in 1862, No. 5: Part of the Iron Bridge near 8th Avenue.* 1862.

8. Leopoldo Alinari. *Firenze, Il Battistero.*   c. 1856.

Moving figures inevitably left "ghosts" during the long exposures
required by early photography; posed figures supplied scale and mood.

9. Leopoldo Alinari.   *Siena, Convente di S. Domenico.*   c. 1856.

10. Leopoldo Alinari.   *Bagni di Lucca, Ponte alla Maddalena.*   c. 1856.

11. Édouard-Denis Baldus.   [*View of the Seine, Paris*]. *No. 83*.   c. 1860.

12. Édouard-Denis Baldus. *St. Eustache. Paris No. 37.*   c. 1860.

In this beautifully composed photograph, the triangles of the roofs of
old Les Halles are repeated in the church's flying buttresses.

13. Édouard-Denis Baldus.   [*Palais-Royal*].   c. 1860.

The restless horses have blurred their own images as well as those of the carriages they are pulling.

14. Alvin Langdon Coburn.   *Mr. Longdon's* [*The entrance to Lamb House*].   1907.

15. Alvin Langdon Coburn.   *The Cage [A greengrocer's shop, London].*
1907.

For the frontispieces of Henry James' collected works, the elderly
novelist guided young Coburn on walking tours through the London
neighborhoods of his youth in search of remembered sites and
details—like "the cage."

16. Robert Mieusement. *Château de Chambord, Grande Façade.*   c.1875.

17. Alexander Gardner.   *Ruins of Arsenal, Richmond, Virginia.*   April 1863.

18. Alexander Gardner.   *Studying the Art of War. Fairfax Court House.*
June 1863.

19. Timothy H. O'Sullivan.   *A Harvest of Death, Gettysburg, Pennsylvania.* July 1863.

20. George N. Barnard.   *Trestle Bridge at Whiteside.*   1864.

21. George N. Barnard. *Confederate works front of Atlanta, Ga.* 1864.

22. Albert Fernique. [*Construction of the Statue of Liberty, Workshop view, Paris*]. c. 1880.

The workmen are shaping the copper skin against specially constructed forms.

23. Albert Fernique.   [*Construction of the Statue of Liberty, Courtyard view, Paris*].   c. 1882.

This view shows the surrealistic growth of *Liberty* in the courtyard outside the metalsmiths' workshop.

24. Alfred Stieglitz. *The Steerage.* 1907.

Stieglitz photographed this famous scene aboard a ship en route from New York to Europe. Although it is often thought to depict immigrants arriving in America, the image was intended to be a tonal composition.

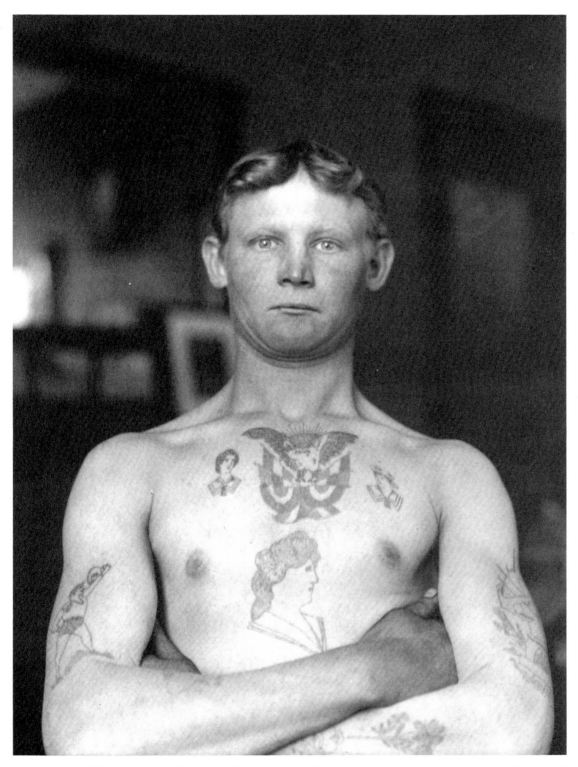

25. Augustus Francis Sherman.   [*Tattooed man, a stowaway from Germany*]. c. 1911.

Sherman was the Chief Registry Clerk at Ellis Island during the peak years of immigration before the First World War.

26. Augustus Francis Sherman.   [*Gypsies from Serbia*].   c. 1910.

27. **Lewis Wickes Hine.** *Street trades, Washington, D.C. N-2945: A 7-year old newsboy who tries to short change customers . . .* April 1912.

28. Lewis Wickes Hine. *Fresh air for the baby, Italian Quarter, New York City.* 1910.

29. Lewis Wickes Hine.   *The Bar-room in a construction camp on New York State Barge Canal.*   1910.

Hine is the progenitor of the great American documentary tradition in twentieth-century photography. Unlike Stieglitz, whose "straight" photography was motivated by a search for a transcendent aesthetic, Hine shared in the spirit of his subjects to produce a moving record of the social reality before his camera.

30. Lewis Wickes Hine.   *The Cast/Behind the Footlights/A Modern Inferno (#325).*   c. 1909.

The men shown here are Pittsburgh steel-workers.

31. Maxime Du Camp. *Ibsamboul, Colosse médial du sphéos de phrè.* [*sic*].   c. 1850.

While still in their twenties, Du Camp and the novelist Gustave Flaubert spent nearly three years touring the Middle East and its archaeological sites.

32. Maxime Du Camp. *Vue Générale* [*Cairo*]. c. 1850.

33. Maxime Du Camp. *Palmiers doum.* c. 1850.

34. Maxime Du Camp.   *Syrie. Baalbeck. Colonnade du temple du soleil.*
c. 1850.

35. Francis Frith. *Colossal Sculptures at Philae.* 1860.

36. Francis Frith.   *The Pyramids of Sakkarah. From the North East.* 1858.

Frith became the most prolific English view photographer and his
popular Middle Eastern views were sold in print shops in England
and America.

37. Francis Frith. *The Approach to Philae.* 1859/60.

The island of Philae was submerged upon completion of the Aswan High Dam in 1971. An international fund facilitated the rescue of most of its monuments.

38. D. Constantin.   *Temple of Jupiter Olympus. Athens.*   c. 1860.

Curiously, the Middle East was much more popular with early expeditionary photographers than the Classical World.

39. Claude-Joseph-Désiré Charnay.   *Grand palais, à Mitla; Intérieur de la cour.*   c. 1858.

Charnay, like Frith in Egypt, made ample use of the ruins' dark interiors to process his plates.

40. Claude-Joseph-Désiré Charnay.   *Palais des nonnes, à Chichen-Itza.*
Façade de l'aile gauche.   c. 1858.

41. Claude-Joseph-Désiré Charnay. *Grand palais, à Mitla; Grande salle.* c. 1858.

42. Louis-Auguste and Auguste-Rosalie Bisson.   [*Ascending Mont Blanc*].   c. 1862.

43. Charles Leander Weed. *Sugar Loaf—Little Yo-Semite Valley.* c. 1864/65.

Though Weed made the very first photographs in Yosemite, it was the mammoth views by his rival Watkins that helped establish Yosemite as a protected natural area.

44. Charles Leander Weed.   *Three Brothers.*   c. 1864/65.

45. Charles Leander Weed.   *The Valley, from the Mariposa Trail.*
c. 1864/65.

46. Charles Leander Weed. *Cathedral Rocks.*   c. 1864/65.

47. Carleton E. Watkins.   *Section of Grizzly Giant, Mariposa Grove 33 ft. diameter No.113.*   c. 1866.

The Grizzly Giant is really a double portrait, of the tree and of the park's venerable custodian.

48. Carleton E. Watkins. *Mirror View, El Capitan, Yosemite, No. 38.*
c. 1866.

49. Carleton E. Watkins.   *Up the Valley, Yosemite No. 9.*   c. 1866.

73

50. Carleton E. Watkins.   *The Vernal and Nevada Falls, from Glacier Point, Yosemite, Cal. No.100.*   c. 1866.

51. Andrew Joseph Russell. *Snow and Timber Line, Laramie Mountains.*
1867/68.

Russell was hired by the Union Pacific Railroad to document the construction of America's first transcontinental railway.

52. Andrew Joseph Russell. *The Wind Mill at Laramie.* 1867/68.

53. Andrew Joseph Russell. *Hanging Rock, Foot of Echo Cañon.*
1867/68.

54. Timothy H. O'Sullivan.   *Rock Carved by Drifting Sand, Below Fort-ification Rock, Arizona.*   1871.

55. Timothy H. O'Sullivan.   *Ancient Ruins in the Cañon de Chelle,*
N.M., In a niche 50 feet above present Cañon bed.   1873.

56. William Bell. *Geological Series No. 49: Rain Sculpture, Salt Creek Cañon, Utah.* 1872.

57. William Bell.   *Utah Series No. 10: Hieroglyphic Pass, Opposite Paro-wan, Utah.*   1872.

58. William Bradford, aided by John L. Dunmore and George Critcherson. *Hunting by steam in Melville Bay in August. Killing six polar bears
in one day.* 1869.

59. William Bradford, aided by John L. Dunmore and George Critcherson.   *Kungnait Mountain 4,400 ft. high.*   1869.

60. William Bradford, aided by John L. Dunmore and George Critcherson. *View looking down Karsut Fiord.* 1869.

61. Samuel Bourne. *The Happy Valley. Gwalior.*   1860s.

62. Samuel Bourne. *The Snows from Sandakfoo. Darjeeling.* 1860s.

Unlike his contemporaries in expeditionary photography who traveled to distant lands and then returned to England to work, Bourne settled in India, becoming the subcontinent's leading landscape photographer.

63. John Thomson.   *Ruins. City of Ayuthia, Ancient Capital of Siam.*
c. 1866.

Thomson is famous primarily for his *Illustrations of China and Its People,* but he also photographed throughout Southeast Asia.

64. John Thomson.   *Theatrical Performance, Bangkok.*   c. 1866.

65. John Thomson.   *King of Siam's State Barge.*   c. 1866.

66. Edwin Hale Lincoln.   *Caltha palustris/ Marsh-marigold/ Cowslips.*
1900s.

67. Edwin Hale Lincoln. *Pogonia ophioglossides/Rose pogonia/Snake mouth.*   1900s.

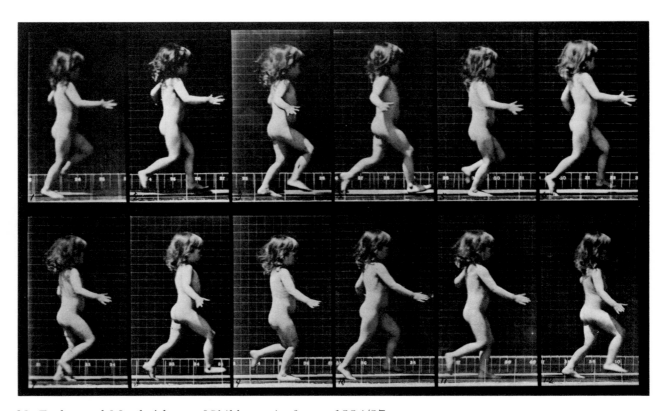

68. Eadweard Muybridge.   [*Child running*].   c. 1884/87.

Muybridge's motion studies prefigured the development of early
motion-picture technology.

69. Eadweard Muybridge.   [*Cockatoo flying*].   c. 1884/87.

A Zuñi eagle cage.

Hillers, photo.

70. John K. Hillers. *A Zuñi eagle cage.* c. 1875.

Only about thirty years separate Hillers' ethnographic records of a still vital culture from Curtis' and Moon's interpretive studies of a vanishing way of life and its people.

71. John K. Hillers.   *Terraced houses at Wolpi.*   c. 1875.

Zuñi watching.   Hillers, phot

72. John K. Hillers.   *Zuñi Watching.*   c. 1875.

73. Edward Sheriff Curtis. *Cañon del Muerte—Navajo No. 421-06.*
c. 1900.

74. Edward Sheriff Curtis.   *"The Vanishing Race" no. 378.*   c. 1900.
This is one of Curtis' rare allegories.

75. Edward Sheriff Curtis.   *Housetop Life—Hopi.*   c. 1900.

76. Karl E. Moon. *The Kivas of Walpi.* 1907.

77. Karl E. Moon. *Nampeyo (Painting Pottery).*   c. 1910.

78. Karl E. Moon. *"Tong Pah"—Taos.* c. 1909.

79. Juan Laurent. *Cordova—Les laveuses.* c. 1868.

80. *Attrib*. Felice Antonio Beato.   [*Prince Okudaira*].   c. 1867.

Beato's single-figure genre studies are delicately hand-colored, apparently in imitation of Japanese woodcuts.

81. *Attrib.* Felice Antonio Beato.   *Coolie.*   c. 1867.

82. *Attrib.* Felice Antonio Beato.   *Woman Using Cosmetics.*   c. 1867.

83. *Attrib.* Felice Antonio Beato.   *Woman in Winter Dress.*   c. 1867.

84. Frank Meadow Sutcliffe. *The Bathers. FMS 104.* 1880s.

Sutcliffe spent his adult life in Whitby on the English Channel, documenting the fishing village, its inhabitants, and the surrounding countryside in a manner at once pictorial and naturalistic.

85. Frank Meadow Sutcliffe.   *"Give us a lift." FMS 169.*   1880s.

86. Frank Meadow Sutcliffe. *"There she goes." FMS 121.* 1880s.

87. Frank Meadow Sutcliffe.   [*Whitby fishermen beaching a boat*]. *FMS 26.*
1880s.

88. Mathew B. Brady.   [*Committee on the Fine Arts of the New York Metropolitan Fair, for the U.S. Sanitary Commission*].   1864.

The artists and patrons who participated in the major Union fundraising effort during the Civil War are grouped around their specialties or favorite media. Only Brady looks out toward the camera.

89. Mathew B. Brady.   *The Fairy Wedding Party. Mr. & Mrs. Genl. Tom Thumb, Commodore Nutt and Miss Minnie Warren.*   1863.

90. Etienne Carjat. *Charles Baudelaire.*   c. 1863.

91. Etienne Carjat.   *Henri Monnier.*   c. 1860.

Monnier (1805–1877) was a man of many rôles—author, illustrator of La Fontaine, and sometime actor.

92. George Bernard Shaw.   [*Self-portrait at the piano*].   1903.

Shaw wrote to his friend Frederick H. Evans on the verso: "GBS on Xmas Day 1903, 3 minutes exposure—pretty steady for his age—eh."

93. George Bernard Shaw.   [*Self-portrait*].   1899.

94. Edward Steichen.　[*Alfred Stieglitz*].　1905.

95. Alfred Stieglitz.   [*Hands of Georgia O'Keeffe*].   c. 1918.

96. Alfred Stieglitz. [*Hands of Georgia O'Keeffe*]. c. 1918.

Catalog of Plates

Note: Photograph titles supplied by the editor are in brackets. Dimensions are given in millimeters, height before width. Works that are smaller than the format of this book have been reproduced in their exact size; larger images had to be reduced.

1. William Henry Fox Talbot (English, 1800–1877). [*Photogenic drawing of a plant*]. c. 1845. Salt print from paper negative. 231 x 192 mm. John Shaw Billings Memorial Collection, 1938. Similar to but not the same as Plate VII in *The Pencil of Nature.*

2. William Henry Fox Talbot (English, 1800–1877). [*China on two shelves*]. c. 1841–1843. Salt print from paper negative. 156 x 193 mm. John Shaw Billings Memorial Collection, 1938. Similar to but not the same as Plate III in *The Pencil of Nature.*

3. William Henry Fox Talbot (English, 1800–1877). [*Nelson Column under construction, Trafalgar Square*]. c. 1845. Salt print from paper negative. 188 x 231 mm. John Shaw Billings Memorial Collection, 1938.

4. William Langenheim (American, b. Germany, 1807–1874). Frederick Langenheim (American, b. Germany, 1809–1879). *Niagara Falls . . . General View from American Side.* 1855. Hand-colored albumen on glass stereograph. Image 66 x 60 mm. Robert Dennis Collection of Stereoscopic Views, 1940.

5. William Langenheim (American, b. Germany, 1807–1874). Frederick Langenheim (American, b. Germany, 1809–1879). *New York City and Vicinity. View from Peter Cooper's Institute towards Astor Place.* c. 1856. Hand-colored albumen on glass stereograph. Image 63 x 59 mm. Robert Dennis Collection of Stereoscopic Views, 1940.

6. Victor Prevost (American, b. France, 1820–1881). *Central Park in 1862, No. 17: Bird's Nest* [*Bethesda Fountain Stairway*]. 1862. Albumen print, signed in negative, photographer's blind-stamp on mount and print. 142 x 138 mm. Robert L. Stuart Collection, 1892.

7. Victor Prevost (American, b. France, 1820–1881). *Central Park in 1862, no. 5: Part of the Iron Bridge near 8th Avenue.* 1862. Albumen print, signed in negative, photographer's blind-stamp on

mount and print. 140 x 141 mm. Robert L. Stuart Collection, 1892.

8. Leopoldo Alinari (Italian, 1832–1865). *Firenze, Il Battistero.* c. 1856. Albumen print. 333 x 253 mm. Source unknown, 1914.

9. Leopoldo Alinari (Italian, 1832–1865). *Siena, Convente di S. Domenico.* c. 1856. Albumen print. 338 x 253 mm. Source unknown, 1914.

10. Leopoldo Alinari (Italian, 1832–1865). *Bagni di Lucca, Ponte alla Maddalena.* c. 1856. Albumen print. 258 x 339 mm. Source unknown, 1914.

11. Édouard-Denis Baldus (French, 1820–1882). [*View of the Seine, Paris*]. *No. 83.* c. 1860. Albumen print, photographer's ink stamp on mount. 342 x 436 mm. Source unknown, 1914.

12. Édouard-Denis Baldus (French, 1820–1882). *St. Eustache. Paris No. 37.* c. 1860. Albumen print, photographer's ink stamp on mount. 427 x 338 mm. Source unknown, 1914.

13. Édouard-Denis Baldus (French, 1820–1882). [*Palais-Royal*]. c. 1860. Albumen print, photographer's ink stamp on mount. 340 x 444 mm. Source unknown, 1914.

14. Alvin Langdon Coburn (American, 1882–1966). *Mr. Longdon's* [*The entrance to Lamb House*]. 1907. Photogravure. 110 x 86 mm. From *The Novels and Tales of Henry James*, Vol. 9, "The Awkward Age" (New York: Scribner's, 1908). Source unknown, n.d.

15. Alvin Langdon Coburn (American, 1882–1966). *The Cage* [*A Greengrocer's shop, London*]. 1907. Photogravure. 125 x 73 mm. From *The Novels and Tales of Henry James*, Vol. 11, "In the Cage" (New York: Scribner's, 1908). Source unknown, n.d.

16. Robert Mieusement (French, active c. 1875). *Château de Chambord, Grande Façade.* c. 1875. Albumen print on letterpress mount. 250 x 351 mm. From: *Les Châteaux historiques: Chambord* (Paris: Ducher, 1875). Astor Library.

17. Alexander Gardner (American, b. Scotland, 1821–1882). *Ruins of Arsenal, Richmond, Virginia.* April 1863. Albumen print on letterpress mount. 172 x 225 mm. Plate 91 of *Gardner's Photographic Sketch-Book of the War* (Washington, 1865–1866). Source unknown, n.d.

18. Alexander Gardner (American, b. Scotland, 1821–1882). *Studying the Art of War. Fairfax Court House.* June 1863. Albumen print on letterpress mount. 177 x 229 mm. Plate 45 of *Gardner's Photographic Sketch-Book of the War* (Washington, 1865–1866). Source unknown, n.d.

19. Timothy H. O'Sullivan (American, b. Ireland?, c. 1840–1882). *A Harvest of Death, Gettysburg, Pennsylvania.* July 1863. Albumen print on letterpress mount. 172 x 224 mm. Plate 36 of *Gardner's Photographic Sketch-Book of the War* (Washington, 1865–1866). Source unknown, n.d.

20. George N. Barnard (American, 1819–1902). *Trestle Bridge at Whiteside.* 1864. Albumen print. 255 x 355 mm. Same as Plate 4 of *Photographic Views of Sherman's Campaign* (New York: Press of Wynkoop & Hallenbeck, 1866). Emmet Collection, 1902.

21. George N. Barnard (American, 1819–1902). *Confederate works front of Atlanta, Ga.* 1864. Albumen print on contemporary mount with mss title. 254 x 354 mm. Same as Plate 43, "Rebel Works in Front of Atlanta, Ga., No. 5," of *Photographic Views of Sherman's Campaign* (New York: Press of Wynkoop & Hallenbeck, 1866). Emmet Collection, 1902.

22. Albert Fernique (French, active c. 1870–1904). [*Construction of the Statue of Liberty, Workshop view, Paris*]. c. 1880. Albumen print, photographer's blind-stamp on mount. 378 x 463 mm. From *Album des travaux de construction de la statue colossale de la Liberté destinée au port de New-York* (Paris, 1883). Purchase, 1938.

23. Albert Fernique (French, active c. 1870–1904). [*Construction of the Statue of Liberty, Courtyard view, Paris*]. c. 1882. Albumen print, photographer's blind-stamp on mount. 446 x 267 mm. From *Album des travaux de construction de la statue colossale de la Liberté destinée au port de New-York* (Paris, 1883). Purchase, 1938.

24. Alfred Stieglitz (American, 1864–1946). *The Steerage.* 1907. Photogravure. 333 x 262 mm. From *291* no. 7–8 (New York: September–October 1915). Purchase, 1915.

25. Augustus Francis Sherman (American, c. 1865–1925). [*Tattooed man, a stowaway from Germany*]. c. 1911. Silver print, mounted by the photographer. 240 x 174 mm. Bequest of William Williams, 1947.

26. Augustus Francis Sherman (American, c. 1865–1925). [*Gypsies from Serbia*]. c. 1910. Silver print, mounted by the photographer. 240 x 171 mm. Bequest of William Williams, 1947.

27. Lewis Wickes Hine (American, 1874–1940). *Street trades, Washington, D.C. N-2945: A 7-year old newsboy who tries to short change customers . . .* April 1912. Silver print c. 1940; titled and captioned on mount by the photographer: *Photo-study by Lewis W. Hine.* 166 x 236 mm. Gift of the Russell Sage Foundation Library, n.d.

28. Lewis Wickes Hine (American, 1874–1940). *Fresh air for the baby, Italian Quarter, New York City.* 1910. Silver print c. 1940; titled and captioned on mount by the photographer: *Photo-study by Lewis W. Hine.* 118 x 168 mm. Gift of the Russell Sage Foundation Library, n.d.

29. Lewis Wickes Hine (American, 1874–1940). *The Bar-room in a construction camp on New York State Barge Canal.* 1910. Silver print c. 1940; titled and captioned on mount by the photographer: *Photo-study by Lewis W. Hine.* 120 x 172 mm. Gift of the Russell Sage Foundation Library, n.d.

30. Lewis Wickes Hine (American, 1874–1940). *The Cast/Behind the Footlights/A Modern Inferno (#325).* c. 1909. Silver print, ms. title on verso. 117 x 170 mm. Gift of Garrett and Ralph Oppenheim (James Oppenheim Papers), 1944.

31. Maxime Du Camp (French, 1822–1894). *Ibsamboul, Colosse médial du sphéos de phrè* [*sic*]. c. 1850. Albumen print from a paper negative, on letterpress mount. 211 x 167 mm. Plate 106 of *Égypte, Nubie, Palestine et Syrie* (Paris: Gide et J. Baudry, 1852). Astor Library.

32. Maxime Du Camp (French, 1822–1894). *Vue Générale* [*Cairo*]. c. 1850. Albumen print from a paper negative, on letterpress mount. 156 x 209 mm. Plate 1 of *Égypte, Nubie, Palestine et Syrie* (Paris: Gide et J. Baudry, 1852). Astor Library.

33. Maxime Du Camp (French, 1822–1894). *Palmiers doum.* c. 1850. Albumen print from a paper negative, on letterpress mount. 165 x 209 mm. Plate 22 of *Égypte, Nubie, Palestine et Syrie* (Paris: Gide et J. Baudry, 1852). Astor Library.

34. Maxime Du Camp (French, 1822–1894). *Syrie. Baalbeck. Colonnade du temple du soleil.* c. 1850. Albumen print from a paper negative, on letterpress mount. 167 x 220 mm. Plate 121 of *Égypte, Nubie, Palestine et Syrie* (Paris: Gide et J. Baudry, 1852). Astor Library.

35. Francis Frith (English, 1822–1898). *Colossal Sculptures at Philae.* 1860. Albumen print on letterpress mount. 220 x 160 mm. From *Upper Egypt and Ethiopia* (London: James S. Virtue). Purchase, 1929.

36. Francis Frith (English, 1822–1898). *The Pyramids of Sakkarah. From the North East.* 1858. Albumen print on letterpress mount. 164 x 230 mm. From *Lower Egypt, Thebes and the Pyramids of Egypt* (London: James S. Virtue). Purchase, 1929.

37. Francis Frith (English, 1822–1898). *The Approach to Philae.* 1859/60. Albumen print on letterpress mount. 163 x 223 mm. From *Upper Egypt and Ethiopia* (London: James S. Virtue). Purchase, 1929.

38. D. Constantin (Greek, active c. 1850–c. 1870). *Temple of Jupiter Olympus. Athens*. c. 1860. Albumen print on mount with manuscript title. 280 x 378 mm. Gift of Mrs. George Bliss, 1934.

39. Claude-Joseph-Désiré Charnay (French, 1828–1915). *Grand palais, à Mitla; Intérieur de la cour*. c. 1858. Albumen print on letterpress mount. 275 x 409 mm. Plate 11 of *Cités et ruines américaines* (Paris: Gide, 1862). Astor Library.

40. Claude-Joseph-Désiré Charnay (French, 1828–1915). *Palais des nonnes, à Chichen-Itza. Façade de l'aile gauche*. c. 1858. Albumen print, signed in the negative, on letterpress mount. 420 x 340 mm. Plate 28 of *Cités et ruines américaines* (Paris: Gide, 1862). Astor Library.

41. Claude-Joseph-Désiré Charnay (French, 1828–1915). *Grand palais, à Mitla; Grande salle*. c. 1858. Albumen print on letterpress mount. 269 x 406 mm. Plate 10 of *Cités et ruines américaines* (Paris: Gide, 1862). Astor Library.

42. Louis-Auguste Bisson (French, 1814–1876). Auguste-Rosalie Bisson (French, 1826–1900). [*Ascending Mont Blanc*]. c. 1862. Albumen print with blind stamp. 393 x 227 mm. Source unknown, 1928.

43. Charles Leander Weed (American, 1824–1903). *Sugar Loaf—Little Yo-Semite Valley*. c. 1864/65. Albumen print, signed in pencil on mount with letterpress title label. 540 x 439 mm. Gift of Albert Boni, 1952.

44. Charles Leander Weed (American, 1824–1903). *Three Brothers*. c. 1864/65. Albumen print, signed in pencil on mount with letterpress title label. 427 x 535 mm. Gift of Albert Boni, 1952.

45. Charles Leander Weed (American, 1824–1903). *The Valley, from the Mariposa Trail*. c. 1864/65. Albumen print, signed in pencil on mount with letterpress title label. 438 x 536 mm. Gift of Albert Boni, 1952.

46. Charles Leander Weed (American, 1824–1903). *Cathedral Rocks*. c. 1864/65. Albumen print, signed in pencil on mount with letterpress title label. 448 x 535 mm. Gift of Albert Boni, 1952.

47. Carleton E. Watkins (American, 1829–1916). *Section of Grizzly Giant, Mariposa Grove 33 ft. diameter No. 113*. c. 1866. Albumen print, signed and titled on print verso in pencil. 521 x 395 mm. Source unknown, 1934.

48. Carleton E. Watkins (American, 1829–1916). *Mirror View, El Capitan, Yosemite No. 38*. c. 1866. Albumen print, signed and numbered in ink on mount, titled in pencil. 525 x 399 mm. Gift of Albert Boni, 1952.

49. Carleton E. Watkins (American, 1829–1916). *Up the Valley, Yosemite No. 9*. c. 1866. Albumen print, signed and numbered in ink on mount, titled in pencil. 398 x 525 mm. Gift of Albert Boni, 1952.

50. Carleton E. Watkins (American, 1829–1916). *The Vernal and Nevada Falls, from Glacier Point, Yosemite, Cal. No.100*. c. 1866. Albumen print, published by I. W. Taber of San Francisco. 393 x 520 mm. Gift of Charles W. McAlpin, 1935.

51. Andrew Joseph Russell (American, 1830–1902). *Snow and Timber Line, Laramie Mountains*. 1867/68. Albumen print on letterpress mount. 235 x 301 mm. Plate 13 of *The Great West Illustrated* (New York: Union Pacific Railroad, 1869). Samuel J. Tilden Collection, 1895.

52. Andrew Joseph Russell (American, 1830–1902). *The Wind Mill at Laramie*. 1867/68. Albumen print on letterpress mount. 223 x 308 mm. Plate 16 of *The Great West Illustrated* (New York: Union Pacific Railroad, 1869). Samuel J. Tilden Collection, 1895.

53. Andrew Joseph Russell (American, 1830–1902). *Hanging Rock, Foot of Echo Cañon*. 1867/68. Albumen print on letterpress mount. 233 x 301 mm. Plate 32 of *The Great West Illustrated* (New York: Union Pacific Railroad, 1863). Samuel J. Tilden Collection, 1865.

54. Timothy H. O'Sullivan (American, b. Ireland?, 1840–1882). *Rock Carved by Drifting Sand, Below Fortification Rock, Arizona*. 1871. Albumen print on letterpress mount. 202 x 272 mm. From *Photographs Showing Landscapes, Geological and Other Features . . . Obtained in Connection with Geographical and Geological Explorations and Surveys West of the 100th Meridian . . .* (Washington: War Dept.). Gift of Dr. John Shaw Billings, 1898.

55. Timothy H. O'Sullivan (American, b. Ireland?, 1840–1882). *Ancient Ruins in the Cañon de Chelle, N.M., In a niche 50 feet above present Cañon bed*. 1873. Albumen print on letterpress mount. 268 x 202 mm. From *Photographs Showing Landscapes, Geological and Other Features . . . Obtained in Connection with Geographical and Geological Explorations and Surveys West of the 100th Meridian . . .* (Washington: War Dept.). Gift of Dr. John Shaw Billings, 1898.

56. William Bell (American, c. 1830–1910). *Geological Series No. 49: Rain Sculpture, Salt Creek Cañon, Utah*. 1872. Albumen print on letterpress mount. 283 x 204 mm. Gift of Dr. John Shaw Billings, 1910.

57. William Bell (American, c. 1830–1910). *Utah Series No. 10: Hieroglyphic Pass, Opposite Parowan, Utah*. 1872. Albumen print on letterpress mount. 231 x 182 mm. Gift of Dr. John Shaw Billings, 1910.

58. William Bradford (American, 1823–1892). Aided by John L. Dunmore and George Critcherson. *Hunting by steam in Melville Bay in August. Killing six polar bears in one day*. 1869. Albumen print. 285 x 392 mm. Same as plate 83 in Bradford's *The Arctic Regions* (1873). Robert L. Stuart Collection, 1892.

59. William Bradford (American, 1823–1892). Aided by John L. Dunmore and George Critcherson. *Kungnait Mountain 4,400 ft. high.* 1869. Albumen print. 293 x 406 mm. Same as plate 49 in Bradford's *The Arctic Regions* (1873). Robert L. Stuart Collection, 1892.

60. William Bradford (American, 1823–1892). Aided by John L. Dunmore and George Critcherson. *View looking down Karsut Fiord.* 1869. Albumen print. 291 x 385 mm. Similar to the view published as plate 62/63 in Bradford's *The Arctic Regions* (1873). Robert L. Stuart Collection, 1892.

61. Samuel Bourne (English, 1834–1912). *The Happy Valley. Gwalior.* 1860s. Albumen print, signed and numbered in negative. 217 x 274 mm. Source unknown, 1953.

62. Samuel Bourne (English, 1834–1912). *The Snows from Sandakfoo. Darjeeling.* 1860s. Albumen print, signed and numbered in negative. 181 x 287 mm. Source unknown, 1953.

63. John Thomson (Scottish, 1837–1921). *Ruins. City of Ayuthia, Ancient Capital of Siam.* c. 1866. Albumen print tipped to album leaf with mss. title. 220 x 163 mm. Anonymous gift, 1968.

64. John Thomson (Scottish, 1837–1921). *Theatrical Performance, Bangkok.* c. 1866. Albumen print signed in negative, tipped to album leaf with mss. title. 187 x 230 mm. Anonymous gift, 1968.

65. John Thomson (Scottish, 1837–1921). *King of Siam's State Barge.* c. 1866. Albumen prints joined on album leaf with mss. title. 158 x 434 mm together. Anonymous gift, 1968.

66. Edwin Hale Lincoln (American, 1848–1938). *Caltha palustris/ Marsh-marigold/ Cowslips.* 1900s. Platinum print on letterpress mount. 237 x 187 mm. Plate 12 of *Wild Flowers of New England,* Part I (Pittsfield, Mass., 1910). Anna Palmer Draper Fund, 1912.

67. Edwin Hale Lincoln (American, 1848–1938). *Pogonia ophioglossides/ Rose pogonia/ Snake mouth.* 1900s. Platinum print on letterpress mount. 234 x 185 mm. Plate 158 of *Wild Flowers of New England,* Part VII (Pittsfield, Mass., 1910). Anna Palmer Draper Fund, 1912.

68. Eadweard Muybridge (English, active America, 1830–1904). *[Child running].* c. 1884/87. Collotype, letterpress plate. 201 x 327 mm. Plate 469 of *Animal Locomotion,* Vol. VI (Philadelphia: University of Pennsylvania, 1887). Gift of Alexander Maitland, 1895.

69. Eadweard Muybridge (English, active America, 1830–1904). *[Cockatoo flying].* c. 1884/87. Collotype, letterpress plate. 200 x 360 mm. Plate 762 of *Animal Locomotion,* Vol. XI (Philadelphia: University of Pennsylvania, 1887). Gift of Alexander Maitland, 1895.

70. John K. Hillers (American, b. Germany, 1843–1925). *A Zuñi eagle cage.* c. 1875. Albumen print, signed and titled on negative, letterpress mount. 183 x 230 mm. Wilberforce Eames Indian Collection, 1912.

71. John K. Hillers (American, b. Germany, 1843–1925). *Terraced houses at Wolpi.* c. 1875. Albumen print, signed and titled on negative, on letterpress mount. 250 x 328 mm. Wilberforce Eames Indian Collection, 1912.

72. John K. Hillers (American, b. Germany, 1843–1925). *Zuñi Watching.* c. 1875. Albumen print, signed and titled on negative, on letterpress mount. 230 x 184 mm. Wilberforce Eames Indian Collection, 1912.

73. Edward Sheriff Curtis (American, 1868–1952). *Cañon del Muerte—Navajo No. 421-06.* c. 1900. Silver print, signed, on photographer's mount with title. 412 x 308 mm. Source unknown, n.d.

74. Edward Sheriff Curtis (American, 1868–1952). *"The Vanishing Race" no. 378.* c. 1900. Silver print, signed, on photographer's mount with label on verso. 380 x 517 mm. Source unknown, n.d.

75. Edward Sheriff Curtis (American, 1868–1952). *Housetop Life—Hopi.* c. 1900. Silver print, signed, on photographer's mount with title. 402 x 305 mm. Source unknown, n.d.

76. Karl E. Moon (American, b. Germany, 1878–1948). *The Kivas of Walpi.* 1907. Silver print. 413 x 330 mm. Source unknown, 1940.

77. Karl E. Moon (American, b. Germany, 1878–1948). *Nampeyo (Painting Pottery).* c. 1910. Silver print. 343 x 417 mm. Source unknown, 1940.

78. Karl E. Moon (American, b. Germany, 1878–1948). *"Tong Pah"—Taos.* c. 1909. Silver print. 414 x 290 mm. Source unknown, 1940.

79. Juan Laurent (Spanish, active c. 1868–c. 1880). *Cordova—Les laveuses.* c. 1868. Albumen print on letterpress mount. 341 x 250 mm. From *Museos de España* (Madrid, Paris: J. Laurent y Cia.). Source unknown, n.d.

80. *Attrib.* Felice Antonio Beato (English, b. Italy, d. Egypt, active c. 1850–1903). *[Prince Okudaira].* c. 1867. Hand-colored albumen print, on album leaf with descriptive label. 278 x 229 mm. From a published album, now lacking title (Yokohama, 1868). Gift of Miss E. F. Thomas, 1924.

81. *Attrib.* Felice Antonio Beato (English, b. Italy, d. Egypt, active c. 1850–1903). *Coolie.* c. 1867. Hand-colored albumen print, on album leaf with descriptive label. 286 x 238 mm. From a published album, now lacking title (Yokohama, 1868). Gift of Miss E. F. Thomas, 1924.

82. *Attrib.* Felice Antonio Beato (English, b. Italy, d. Egypt, active c. 1850–1903). *Woman Using Cosmetics.* c. 1867. Hand-colored albumen print, on album leaf with descriptive label. 200 x 254 mm. From a published album, now lacking title (Yokohama, 1868). Gift of Miss E. F. Thomas, 1924.

83. *Attrib.* Felice Antonio Beato (English, b. Italy, d. Egypt, active c. 1850–1903. *Woman in Winter Dress*. c. 1867. Hand-colored albumen print, on album leaf with descriptive label. 295 x 244 mm. From a published album, now lacking title (Yokohama, 1868). Gift of Miss E. F. Thomas, 1924.

84. Frank Meadow Sutcliffe (English, 1853–1941). *The Bathers*. FMS 104. 1880s. Carbon print, initialed and numbered in negative. 146 x 203 mm. From *Frank M. Sutcliffe's Photographs*, a photo album. Gift of Stephen Clark, 1939.

85. Frank Meadow Sutcliffe (English, 1853–1941). *"Give us a lift."* FMS 169. 1880s. Carbon print, initialed and numbered in negative. 180 x 157 mm. From *Frank M. Sutcliffe's Photographs*, a photo album. Gift of Stephen Clark, 1939.

86. Frank Meadow Sutcliffe (English, 1853–1941). *"There she goes,"* FMS 121. 1880s. Carbon print, initialed and numbered in negative. 196 x 145 mm. From *Frank M. Sutcliffe's Photographs*, a photo album. Gift of Stephen Clark, 1939.

87. Frank Meadow Sutcliffe (English, 1853–1941). *[Whitby fishermen beaching a boat]*. FMS 26. 1880s. Carbon print, initialed and numbered in negative. 145 x 197 mm. From *Frank M. Sutcliffe's Photographs*, a photo album. Gift of Stephen Clark, 1939.

88. Mathew B. Brady (American, c. 1823–1896). *[Committee on the Fine Arts of the New York Metropolitan Fair, for the U.S. Sanitary Commission]*. 1864. Albumen print. 149 x 231 mm. From *Recollections of the Art Exhibition, Metropolitan Fair, New York, April 1864* (New York: M. B. Brady, 1864). Robert L. Stuart Collection, 1892.

89. Mathew B. Brady (American, c. 1823–1896). *The Fairy Wedding Party. Mr. & Mrs. Genl. Tom Thumb, Commodore Nutt and Miss Minnie Warren.* 1863. Albumen print, stereograph, published by Edward Anthony, New York. Double image, 75 x 155 mm. Robert Dennis Collection of Stereoscopic Views, 1940.

90. Etienne Carjat (French, 1828–1906). *Charles Baudelaire.* c. 1863. Later Woodburytype on letterpress mount from a negative made about 1863. 232 x 182 mm. From *Album de la galérie contemporaine* (Paris: Revue Illustrée). Transferred from Circulation Department, 1919.

91. Etienne Carjat (French, 1828–1906). *Henri Monnier.* c. 1860. Later Woodburytype on letterpress mount from a negative made about 1860. 238 x 190 mm. From *Album de la galérie contemporaine* (Paris: Revue Illustrée). Transferred from Circulation Department, 1919.

92. George Bernard Shaw (Irish, 1856–1950). *[Self-portrait at the piano]*. 1903. Silver print. 157 x 96 mm. Purchase (Mitchell Kennerley Papers), 1935–41.

93. George Bernard Shaw (Irish, 1856–1950). *[Self-portrait]*. 1899. Platinum print, printed by Frederick H. Evans. 86 x 57 mm. Purchase (Mitchell Kennerley Papers), 1935–41.

94. Edward Steichen (American, b. Luxembourg, 1879–1973). *[Alfred Stieglitz]*. 1905. Platinum print, signed and dated in border. 292 x 221 mm. Purchase (Mitchell Kennerley Papers), 1935–41.

95. Alfred Stieglitz (American, 1864–1946). *[Hands of Georgia O'Keeffe]*. c. 1918. Silver print. 195 x 248 mm. Purchase (Mitchell Kennerley Papers), 1935–41.

96. Alfred Stieglitz (American, 1864–1946). *[Hands of Georgia O'Keeffe]*. c. 1918. Silver print. 203 x 257 mm. Purchase (Mitchell Kennerley Papers), 1935–41.

Index to Plates